for you 'and' her
you support all of
us to use our
purpose'
with
love,
Hope

Rush

Embracing your purpose and all of the
psychological thrillers it brings with it

Hope LeNoir

Owner of Rise and Fly®, LLC

Rise and Fly ©, LLC
800 East Lamar Blvd. Suite 173
Arlington, TX 76011
www.riseandfly.net

Ordering Information:
Quantity sales. Titles are available for bulk purchases for business, educational, fund raising or sales promotional use. For details, contact the publisher at the address above.
Orders by U.S. trade bookstores and wholesalers.

SECOND EDITION

ISBN-13: 978-1511505581
ISBN-10: 1511505583

To my father, angelic mother and all of the influencers in my bloodline. You made this possible and you helped make this happen. To my closest and distant friends, you make this worthwhile. To my sister, DiAnne, for setting me up to fly.

TABLE OF CONTENTS

Introduction

For some, finding your life purpose is clear as a child. For others, finding your life purpose as a child is far from being clear. Then there are those who were stuck between confusion and clarity as a child *and* as an adult. Your gifted purpose may have come with small hints that, given the level of life experiences, just don't seem to add up. Your gifted purpose made you hungry for something you couldn't pinpoint until you grew into clarity and acceptance. For me, finding my life's gifted purpose wasn't clear until I identified what it is I want to continue to learn and tell others about.

In my journey and, I hope, in your journey too, we must first be sure not to mistake a life dream with purpose. This doesn't mean your life purpose and your *dreams* can't be aligned. Second, your gifted purpose should be in line with your successes, however, understand perception of success does not always demonstrate your gifted purpose. Also, understand your perception of failure does not mean what you're doing is not your purpose, especially if you are driven even more to learn and grow from that perception of failure. I'd like for you to join me as I take you through my journey of discovering and embracing my gifted purpose and all of the psychological thrillers it brings with it.

Instruction to Go Into the Tunnel

"You have to be still," he said. And I tried. I really tried, but it was so cold in that dark and noisy tunnel. I swallowed and took a deep breath. I clutched my entire body with every ounce of cooperation I had left and tried to be very still. Still, *very* still. I focused on the instructions given to me. It felt like ice was taking up the space in my veins all while hugging my arms and thighs. The technician left the room, stood behind the glass wall and turned the switch. The machine that housed my stiff body slid into the darkness of the tunnel. I tried, I really tried not to move, but it was so cold. I couldn't breathe out because he told me to hold my breath and I obeyed. I was so cold and wanted to shiver, but I didn't. I was obedient. As you will read more of my story, you will find I usually obey. The tunnel was dark and I felt, empty I guess. Though I felt everything physically, I have no emotional feeling or maybe I just didn't know how to feel. It wasn't until years later that a neurologist explained to me because of my disease, I don't feel emotions the *usual* way. On this day, I am cocooned in the white tube, engulfed by darkness, shuddering emotionless from the cold. I didn't cry. I didn't feel depression. I didn't feel whatever else some people would have thought healthy for me to feel emotionally. I just simply thought of the cold.

Being engulfed in a white tube begins the story of how I found my gifted purpose, as some call it. As I interpret it, researchers the "feel of gifted purpose" an element of FLOW. Some Spiritualist call it passion. The standard term is purpose. Physiologists may call it logic. Strangers call it plain creepy. I call it all of the above with an added sense of a RUSH. You will recognize that "it," whatever you decide to term it, exists because we each have at least one gifted purpose that brings along with it, a certain sensation. In this book, I will take you on *my* journey of discovery. In the words of a local pastor, my story is personal, but not private, so I am excited to share my journey of discovery with all of you. Perhaps you taking this journey with me will be a time of discovery for you too.

Now, back to the tunnel. The reason I was in the tunnel in the first place was because I woke up blurry eyed one morning. I remember I rubbed my eyes that morning, washed my face and put on my glasses. Dumb glasses. At that moment, I knew the glasses weren't doing their job.

What's the purpose of buying new glasses with supposedly good prescription only to put them on and see everything a blur, like a filthy windshield after going through the rain? My blurred vision went on for days. For days, I drove back and forth, 40 minutes each way, to the volunteer group at a hospital. For some reason, I didn't worry about my sight. It had to be the prescription in these glasses. *Jeez, these glasses.* Lucky for me, all I had to do during my volunteer time was sit in front of the hospital entry way, greet visitors as they came in and let them know what room their loved one was resting.

One day while sitting at the front desk, I realized my vision had gotten worse. I couldn't see the names only twelve inches in front of me.

"Will you help me read this? My eyes are really bothering me today," I said to the volunteer next to me.

"Sure," my co-volunteer said while looking over my shoulder. "I had problems with my eyes too," she continued. "My eye doctor gave me something to clear that right up."

"What was it?"

"Allergies."

By the time I made it back home, I looked up and dialed an eye doctor right away. My *right away* meant 30 minutes of glass cleaning, moving the phone book back and forth, misdialed numbers and confused people answering my call on the other line. Finally I found and correctly dialed an eye doctor willing and able to see me soon. By the time I entered his parking lot, I was ready to discuss my alleged allergies and question how long the medication would take before I saw results.

On appointment day, I entered a scarce, but pleasant eye doctor's office. The employees greeted me. I sat down in a cushiony chair. I took several tests. No alarming grunts from the assistants. No wondering "hum" from the eye doctor. It was business as usual. My screening is over. I went back to my seat in the waiting area and waited for the doctor to come back with results. All I thought was, I can't wait for these allergy drops.

With no job and obviously no benefits, I hope my optician doesn't give me new glasses. *Just give me some eye drops, and I'll be on my way.*

"Hope," the doctor said.

I stood up.

"I'm gonna refer you to an ophthalmologist."

"A who? Why?"

"Well, he's a really nice guy. He's good at what he does."

Seriously? Nice guy? Good at what he does?

"What do you mean? What's going on?" I said. I guess now what I'm "feeling" is what a doctor would call *anxious.*

"This ophthalmologist will be straight forward with you."

"Why can't *you* tell me? What's happening?"

"I don't want to scare you. This guy will take care of you."

I understand. He's probably a new guy and doesn't understand a lot of what's happening. Maybe the other doctor has a bit more experience about allergies.

I turned to the receptionist, "How much do I owe?"

"Twenty dollars," she smiled. "Don't worry," she attempted to console me, "I know people who are legally blind and they get through life really well."

Legally blind? Oh, this is where this is going. I wonder if legally blind people are just blinder than people with astigmatism like me. I wonder if legally blind people can get better seeing-glasses. I paid, got the ophthalmologist address, got my test results and left. As I left, I only

5

noticed the colors of the traffic signs and not the words. I knew the road home was straight so, I didn't have to make many turns. For that, I am grateful. *When I go to the ophthalmologist, I know I need to have someone with me to help me see. I need someone with me to ask the right questions too,* I thought.

The next time I went to the doctor, I remembered I didn't need to be alone. I asked my cousin, Annie to come to the ophthalmologist office with me. I asked her because she would be the calm, nonjudgmental type. She would avoid stress, assumptions or gossip. Her style is to sit and process, then immediately throw out what didn't matter.

Annie sat next to me as I placed the black spoon over my right eye. "I can only see the left part of the screen," I said.

"Blink," the ophthalmologist instructed. I did.

"Does that help?" the ophthalmologist replied.

"No."

"Read what you can," he replied.

I sighed in an effort to regroup and do my best to follow instructions. I read what I could. I described what I thought was there.

6

"Now cover the left eye," He said. I did. "Now read what you can."

In my attempt to show I was following directions, I focused and swallowed hard, "I can't see anything."

My sight had gone. It was like three fourths of my eye was being covered by something black. The other fourth of my eye saw some kind of light, like something glaring from a slightly cracked door. In other words, it was if I was on the dark side of the room looking at the cracked door where there was a room full of blurry, lighting. The slit of light was so thin, I couldn't see what the doctor was asking me to read in front of me. What was my cousin Annie thinking? Feeling? What was I feeling? What was I supposed to feel?

"Anything?"

"I can't see anything," I said. The room was silent. "It's mostly black," I assured them.

Still silence. In that silence, I remembered a dream I had years ago. In the dream, I was standing at a door in a black room. Everything was blurry. I remembered the darkness didn't scare me. I remembered not knowing where I was and how not knowing didn't affect me. I remembered the blurriness in the dream always confused me then I would suddenly wake up from the dream. But now this is real life and I don't get to just wake up.

This time, it was the ophthalmologist who sighed.

Annie just sat there. I didn't see any object move, so I sensed she was calm. I thought calmness was a really cool place to be. It made me think she was a believer in something bigger than the room and that bigger thing would make sure I was okay. I admire believers who believe in bigger things. They teach me it is okay to simply believe. This was one of the first states where I recalled believing and appreciating that all is well. I knew there was a bigger picture. I knew then I was a part of that bigger picture. Though I thought I believed, I was curious of the details.

The doctor sighed again.

"What?" I asked the doctor.

He rolled close on his little stool. "I want you to get an MRI."

"Why?" I asked. There was a pause. "The other doctor said you would be honest with me," I urged.

"We need to see what's happening," he replied.

"What *could* be happening? Could it be cancer? Is that what you are looking for?"

"We will look for a tumor," he said. I left the conversation there. I felt he needed to gather himself even more than I did.

I paid. I got my results from this test. Annie and I left.

"Do you think I-," I began to ask, but I wasn't allowed to complete the question.

"Nah." Annie said. "You're fine. We're just going to take the MRI," she said so nonchalantly. I always wondered if she had spiritual powers to sense the future and all of its truths. Right now, I hope she did.

Now, back to the story of the cold tunnel. Two additional doctors later, a total of four, here I am, lying in a cold room, on a freezing MRI table. Back and forth, back and forth in the white, cold, loud, tiny tunnel.

LESSON 1: Be in every moment of your life. This doesn't mean you will understand what's happening or why it's happening. Actually, to be in the moment means to notice and to exist with the acknowledgement that you are a part of the moment, that moment is a part of you and every moment, whether you are dreaming or awake, is significant. In this story of my journey, I didn't understand what was happening to me and why, but I later understood I had to appreciate it and know I was a part of a big picture for myself, my God and the people around me.

Rush

Hope LeNoir

Following Directions

One Easter Sunday I sat at the dinner table chattering away and laughing at all the jokes we used to play in the country as little kids.

"You're aunt's been in an accident," said one voice at the table.

"You think she's okay?" asked another.

"Who called?" another chimed in.

"Where are they?" the second voice came back.

I don't even remember who the voices belonged to. I guess that's another caveat of my life. I block or intentionally store a lot of things away. I put them in a safe and lock it all up without caring to memorize a combination or location of the key, because I never cared about opening the safe later. This type of storage is a habit and, in my case, habits have a way of desensitizing my feelings. In the end, I unfortunately store away the important things, sometimes I store the beautiful things away too. In this incident, I remembered everyone was talking, but me. I put away my plate. I picked up my keys.

"It's probably no big deal," I shrugged. "Let's go pick her

up. Who's riding with me?" A pile of people jumped in my car.

I arrived to the accident and found there were so many cars parked everywhere. The fire truck was there. But fire trucks are *always* there, aren't they? Customers from Church's Chicken fast food restaurant stood still in amazement.

There was a woman praying with her arms lifted straight in the air. She was praying.

"Lord!" she hollered out. "You can do it!" she said confidently. Her hands flung everywhere. At that moment, all I heard was her cry out. Nothing or no one else. Not even the wind. Though the day was bright outside, not even the sun.

I don't remember getting out of the car or how I got halfway to my niece's body.

"Jesus!" the hollering woman cried out again. I hope Jesus answers her soon.

Then I saw little feet on the ground. Whose feet are those? They are so little. "Healer!" The hollering woman cried out again. Her hands still in the air.

Saleena. *Those were my niece's feet! Where's my sister?*

14

Why is my aunt crying in the car? Why are Saleena's feet laying in the street?

"Stop," a woman said pushing me back. "Go help our aunt."

"No." I pushed back. "I want to see Saleena. And where is my sister?"

"No. Your aunt needs you."

There was that RUSH. I didn't want or need to cry. I didn't feel anger at that moment. I didn't feel overwhelm. I felt the RUSH.

The RUSH is the excitement regarding anticipated enlightenment. This is the overwhelming feeling of seeing something change, even blossom. The sight of worms getting wings. Peak insight right before the flight of the eagle. It was like the music in the movie scene that welcomes in the bulleted hero or the finely cut heroine. I had to touch my niece Saleena. A voice inside my head instructed me, *All you have to do is touch her.*

"Jesus!" that hollering woman is still screaming. "You can save her!" Yes. Yes. I know *God* can. I just need to touch her. "God!" The hollering woman pointed up high with one hand and held tight to a bible in another. I had to keep walking to Saleena.

"Hope! Stop! Go to your aunt," the other woman screamed out.

Please leave me alone. I know what I'm directed to do. I don't like being around unbelievers. I turned and looked at this woman with no expression, just on a pause.

"Go - see - your - aunt," she dictated to me. Now, I feel. I've never felt so disappointed in my life, but I went and found my aunt, I call her Aunt Wilma. She was sitting in a car that didn't belong to her. She is important too, so I will touch her instead. My aunt is a beautiful 5'9" woman, but I remember her legs dangling out of the side of the car like a small child. Maybe it wasn't a car. Maybe it was a van. I forget the important things. I waded through my other aunts who were rubbing Aunt Wilma's back, her arm, her hands. I took her left hand, because I wanted to rub her hand, too. "It's going to be alright," I said. I'm not sure if she believed me, because she wept. That's what I understand sad or uncertain people do. Maybe this is what all people should do now--weep.

"I don't know if she's going to make it," the woman said as she walked toward me.

"Don't say that," I said calmly. I don't like being around nonbelievers, especially in these situations. I wanted nonbelievers to go away. *For the LORD loves the just and will not forsake his faithful ones. They will be protected forever.* [1]

"I can't take that. I can't live with that," Aunt Wilma wept. Immediately a voice wrapped around me, like a happening over my head. *But He said to me, "My grace is sufficient for you, for my power is made perfect in weakness..."* [2]

I wished my aunt had heard that voice instead.

When I turned my head to the side I saw the ambulance take my niece away. Then it was if I came back to myself. I had to think fast enough to catch up. I had to quickly think strategic enough to because I still had a vision to carry out. *Where's my sister? Where's my nephew, Tryaid? Where's Isaac? Let's go to the hospital. I believe in you, God. I have faith.*

Isaac was standing. He was always standing tall and strong. I found my sister standing, too. Right there in front of the hospital. I thought it foolish my sister had to

---

[1] Psalm 37:28
[2] 2 Corinthians 12:9

stand outside. My sister was holding my nephew tight. Tryaid is okay. His eyes were wide open. His pants soaking wet. I wrapped my arms around my sister's waist and around my nephew's thighs. They both felt good in my arms. They're safe. "I believe," I whispered to my sister. It became a mantra I repeated in the cloud of nonbelievers and suffocating echoes of negative voices. Dirty energy.

"I don't think she'll make it," the unbelievers chanted.

"I believe," I whispered in my sister's ear again and again. I was reminded of the time I was in a bible study and the teacher warned me that people around you can contaminate your faith. It only takes one unbeliever in the mist, he said. *And he did not do many miracles there because of their lack of faith.*[3] I believe. "*I* believe," I whispered. I felt like my sister and I were women half exposed, surrounded by hungry vultures. "It's gonna be alright. I believe," I whispered. The unbelievers kept coming. We kept walking, as if in slow motion, surrounded by monsters who were too afraid to touch us. People kept coming to the hospital. They all stood outside.

---

[3] Matthew 13:58

"She has sickle cell anemia. She'll never make it," an unbeliever said loudly.

There were so many talkers, so many conversations, and so many questions. "What's the baby's social?" a nurse got my sister's attention.

"Hope, can I talk to you?" an unbeliever pulled me to the side. My sister and I separated. I so wanted to be next to my sister. "I've seen things like this happen before," the unbeliever continued. "And it's likely your niece won't make it." The words, "I believe," continued to echo in my mind. "You know that right?" the unbeliever repeated. *Your faith can be tainted by the words of unbelievers*, I thought.

I don't like to be around nonbelievers. I believe. Then I was reminded, *take up the shield of faith, with which you can extinguish all the flaming arrows of the evil one.*[4]

"I'm going back to my sister and nephew now," I said to the unbeliever. Sorry, my dear unbeliever, I turned my back on you. *I believe*, wading through the crowd of nonbelievers. I whispered to my sister. She shook her head "yes."

---

[4] Ephesians 6:16

19

Hope LeNoir

Time had passed and my sister and brother-in-law were asked to come inside of the hospital. The whispers outside of the hospital continued. *And He did not do many miracles there because of their lack of faith.*[5] My niece was declared deceased that day.

My sister's body was heavy. She still stood tall, but heavy. Her eyes dry, but tired. My strong and tall standing brother-in-law entered a bathroom and closed the door. Once inside, it sounded as if he obliterated glass. My nephew's bottom soaked in my arms. He looked around in wonder. Outside of certainty, I didn't know what to feel.

Because I know God only chooses the strong, I knew my sister and her family were strong and I will be strong with them.

At that moment, I realized I knew about this moment months ago. I heard a voice, that prepared me to be better equipped for this moment.

I actually remembered this voice clearly. It spoke to me when my niece, nephew and I went out to dinner at the local Piccadilly. My niece was wearing the beautiful dress I had carefully picked out for her. It was soft yellow and

[5] Matthew 13:58

frilly with puffs and sateen ribbons. We made jokes. We laughed at them, as only we would. I made jokes that I was the aunt of all aunts, since I bought them desserts, even though they didn't finish their dinners. Then things paused. I knew my niece will drop her ice-cream on the front of her dress. I knew she would be anxious about what would happen next. Then, the RUSH and with it came a "voice." The voice said, *Don't make this a big deal. Think about how you would feel when all of this is over.* What I thought was, I didn't want to regret my response to the situation. It was then that things resumed and my niece dropped her ice-cream.

"Uh oh," I said smiling. "The ice-cream dropped on your dress. Let's clean if off so your dress will still be pretty." My nephew sat with big eyes. Wondering. Processing. He then shuffled to the left so I could clean off my niece's dress. "Now. Looks good to me. Want another ice-cream?"

"No," my niece said quietly and shook her head.

"It might be nice to finish with some ice-cream. Are you sure?"

She shook her head again.

As I stood there in the hospital, I thought back to that moment. I'm grateful for the RUSH. The voice that came over me quickly, but quietly. I'm glad today, I didn't look back and think, I wished I hadn't said that to her. I'm glad the last thing I actually said was, "It might be nice to finish with some ice-cream. Are you sure?"

I've made my peace with what happened. Selfishly, I am still hurt that she's gone, but I am glad I followed the directions of the voice I heard in my RUSH. So, now here I am, thinking of my angelic niece and her lively face while I am freezing in a loud rigidly sounding tunnel.

I've been told I may have a tumor. I'm certain I will lose my job. I'm legally blind. My car isn't working. And I'm with a medical technician who told me to be very still, don't even breathe. I go inside the cold white tunnel. Again.

LESSON 2: Be aware of the hints given to you regarding your gift. Also know that awareness can come with confusion. For example, I was told to touch, but I was not told I have the ability to heal. I was told to believe, but not instructed on what to believe. Though not complete, the bottom line here is to be aware. Being aware is knowing the RUSH exists when it does. Be in tune and listen to the instruction you've been given by the RUSH. Recognize it is there. Then let others know how you feel. Give them the opportunity to accept or reject what has been given to you to do or say.

This is not About You

At this particular moment in my life, my experiences were not happening the way I expected them to happen. I did everything I was told to do as a child. I got good grades in elementary and junior high school so I would grow up to be whatever in life I wanted to be. Of course, I wasn't quite sure what that was yet. I got good grades in high school so I could go to a great college. I went to a well-respected, private HBCU in New Orleans and tried hard to stay focused. I got internships during the summer. I graduated with honors and went on to graduate school. I graduated with honors from graduate school.

I did what I was told to do, so here comes the good part, right? After three months of constant searching for that promised career, 350 plus mailed resumes, 75 times listening to "You're overqualified" and 67 more times of "You don't have enough experience," I landed a new job and out of excitement, immediately moved. (Now let's really make this long story even shorter.) I got laid off from my new job after 5 months, the first full-time job I've had since finishing graduate school. This was right before

Hope LeNoir

I begin to face the reality of debt and right after my niece died on Easter Sunday. To top it all off, my car stopped working.

Life wasn't responding how I expected it to respond. In my mind, I welcomed death. Mentally and spiritually I felt I was going nowhere. Physically, I kept moving. When my car stopped working, I walked down the street in a hot black suit and broken high heels to get to a church in the next town.

Soon I began to wake up to what I thought was sticky eye lids *or* simply dirty eyeballs. This is what eventually led me to the "white tunnel." After seeing four doctors and running several tests (including a MRI) I found out I had lost three-fourths of my vision. What had I done? When is the "better" coming? To top it all off, a woman, who I'll call Faithful, from the church I was attending called me and gave me the most painful but helpful knowledge I've ever heard. She said, "This is not about you." Believe it or not, that was the best thing I had ever heard in a long time.

Faithful confirmed that my physical, mental and spiritual journey has a purpose. This story was not just about me.

She was absolutely right. Her statement to me made me recall Job's story. In the biblical story about Job, it wasn't about Job either. What it was about was the billions of people who would come to know, be touched by and become encouraged by Job's story. It was also about validating the wondrous works God is capable of doing. At the end of the story, God healed and blessed Job. In the words of a church member, Job had to go through it to get to it, and so did I. The purpose of these happenings was finally clear to me. It was at this point in my journey that I watched God validate.

"This is *not* about you," the woman on the phone began. She ended the conversation with, "Are you coming to bible study?" Without hesitation or expectation, I did and so did God.

I don't remember the rigorous lesson given by the priest, bishop, preacher or whoever he was, that night, but I do remember Faithful standing up. "Hope is going to have a MRI," she said.

We explained I was losing my sight and the doctors thought I may have a tumor. The pastor of the church beckoned for me to come to the front. A voice appeared in my head, *Is any one of you sick? He should call the elders of the church to pray over him and anoint him with oil in the name of the Lord.*[6] On that note, I hoped the elders would come up front too. They came. All of the believers came. The pastor laid his hand on my head. And me, I was simply hoping he wouldn't put oil on my forehead that will ultimately cause me to break out. The pastor didn't speak to the audience like most preachers do. He spoke with God in great belief. The pastor didn't even speak to me. He didn't speak to the elders either. He didn't speak to the women holding hands or the men kneeling. He didn't even speak to Faithful. He spoke to God.

I wasn't "slain in the spirit." I didn't cry. I didn't speak in tongues. I don't remember what the pastor said and I couldn't hear the words engulfed in the cries and agreeing of the congregation. It was as if I could only see everyone, even with my eyes closed, all around me, standing and kneeling in faith. Though I had physically suffered much and tried to no avail to change my situation, I didn't cry. That night, at bible study, I simply raised my hands to

---

[6] James 15:4

receive. *Lord, I have toiled all night and caught nothing, nevertheless.*[7] I believe. *"Take heart, daughter," He said, "your faith has healed you." And the woman was healed from that moment.*[8]

As I continue to take you through my journey, I'll take you back to where I am-in the white tunnel shaking. I am not shaking of fear, but I am shaking because I am cold.

LESSON 3: The third step is to know your gift is not about just you. Yes, there are rewards with using your gift and living on purpose. For example, I received my sight and sanity a lot early than I otherwise would have. I accepted the greater purpose-this was not just about me. Know your experiences are tied to a picture much larger than you. The experiences associated with your gifted purpose is designed to be used to service the needs of others, you can play a part in helping them live in a fuller way.

---

[7] Luke 5:5
[8] Matthew 9:22

Hope LeNoir

The I-Deserve Mentality

...I tell you the truth, if you have faith as small as a mustard seed, you can say to this mountain, "Move from here to there" and it will move. Nothing will be impossible for you.[9]

By this time in my journey, I have gotten my sight back. And though I was previously laid off, I have job experience under my belt. I have a new career in a new location and am loving every moment of my corporate career. I look forward to getting up every day. I relish in the idea that I am special and nothing can take over what I have gained through my journey.

I had fallen in love with the God that so many called on when I was sick, jobless, broke and probably depressed. I fully trust Him, the decisions He has made and the purpose He has for my life. I appreciate His certainty and His ability to nurture me during my uncertainty. I read and study Him. I am determined to learn from Him and keep serving Him. But, yes there is a "but," one day I looked around and felt as if there was just me. I looked around

---

[9] Matthew 17:20

my home and noticed it was empty. It was dark and it was quiet and in a quick passing thought, I longed for a sweet little card. Wanting a card was only a passing thought, because I knew there was no one, really, to give me a card. Neither was there a *reason* to give me a card. Faithful called again. Remember her? She's the one that told me, "This is not about you." She is always calling. "I have some books for you," she said. She later brought books over, each signed, "Love, Faithful." Tucked among the small stack of books was a card signed by her. God had heard my thoughts, and though fleeting, He granted my wish as if He was saying, "I'm still here." With my gift of books and a card was a note that read, "Delight yourself in the LORD and he will give you the desires of your heart-Psalm 37:4." I was quite delighted by her thoughts.

A few weeks later, I had another fleeting thought while driving to a cousin's house. And since I had survived so many trials, I felt content. I existed and so did the world. And then I literally drove past The Rose Theater on the right side of the road. I reminisced over the days I performed in plays there. There I was a French maid, a princess, a dancer and many, many, many other characters. I thought, just for a fleeting moment, "When I get back on my feet, I'll go see a play at The Rose." That very night in the middle of my sleep, my cousin said Mrs. Wanda wanted me to call her. I hadn't seen her in six years. Mrs. Wanda was a leader at the Theater. She somehow knew I was in my hometown and wanted to let me know she had a theater ticket for the next show waiting just for me at the Rose.

LESSON 4: Develop an *I am worth it* and *I will move forward* mindset. There is truth in "The Secret." Think as you desire your life to be. If you want it, think it. While doing that, remember to study to show yourself approved. Build a relationship with your Higher Power. Know that because God has created you, you have a purpose and he is not stingy with his recognition. Accept *you* are valuable and worthy, that you have something to give, and your gifted purpose is real and needed, no matter how big, small, lonely or illogical it may seem. Better yet, don't think about how big, small or illogical they may seem.

Hope LeNoir

Just Tired

I just got tired. I was simply overwhelmed by my friend's description of her latest dream.

She said bugs were flying everywhere in her dream. Grass was growing all over her body. She wanted it to stop. But there was nothing she could do about it. Somehow her mother showed up. Her mother helped. But the grass kept growing. My friend repeated, "The grass was just growing everywhere. It wouldn't stop growing."

"The good news," I said to her, "is that no matter what is going on in your life, you look to your mother for comfort, protection and reliance. You are assured she can provide that for you. The more disturbing news," I continued, "is you have so many things going on in your life. It is your subconscious trying to tell you, you are a busy bee."

I was tickled pink (or a lighter shade of brown) as I imagined my friend standing before her class for seven straight hours, five days a week. Answering questions. Telling jokes. Giving the angry eye. My mind spanned the idea of her grading papers. That's two and a half hours. Then she would prepare for the next day at school. That's one more hour. She would drive past her home to church. She would help the dance team. Choose costumes. Pick up costumes. Attend bible study. Attend women's meeting. Attend choir rehearsal. Plan the next event. I sighed as I thought about my friend's life. She had three children, no husband. She had a four bedroom home. What my friend didn't have was "time." That lack of time and busyness came out in her dreams. Her having this dream why she called me.

I never professed to be a dream interpreter, however, I do know that dreams are important and I take them very seriously. I study them and with great fascination, I've learned our thoughts have a way of coming to the forefront either (1) through our physical aches, pains and jubilations or (2) vividly through our dreams. I prefer to receive my messages via dreams and physical jubilations over life's aches and pains any day.

In another instance, I later talked to Marion. She has no children. She is married. She and her husband have their own place. Marion had *two* jobs. "I'm okay," she said.

"Okay?" I asked aiming for clarification.

"I took a leave of absence. I had an anxiety attack. I blacked out. My doctor prescribed anti-depressants. So, I'm okay."

I pressed my lips tightly together remembering the time I was justifiably chastised by a fellow co-worker for telling one of my closest friends that she should avoid taking antidepressants. "You're not a doctor," my co-worker reminded me. "Some people do need them."

After remembering that conversation, I sighed. This time I told this friend something different. "Just ask God. He'll tell you just what to do."

Strike three is when the epiphany arrived. One of my co-workers had finally found time to have a Saturday luninner (lun –nee-er). It's what we coined our get-together because it was too late for lunch and too early for dinner. She apologized for not being able to have lunch earlier. Earlier, she didn't have time. Life was busy. Busy job. Busy hubby. Busy family. And well, just with what I call, busy preparing to be busy.

At that moment, I begin to "instruct." I told her of my quiet times with God. The first time I found rest in Him. The first time I heard His voice. How my relationship with

God really excelled once I found the time. I testified of life's trials and triumphs and how, with grabbing and lavishing in time, I was able to grow, understand and appreciate everything that happens in time. Before I knew it, my co-worker was testifying to *me,* too. We both left the restaurant spirit-filled and happy. We made the time for God-for ourselves. We were both restored to the point where we could energetically share God's graciousness.

This was only because we had both found time to rest, listen, prepare, swap testimonies and continue to build and maintain our relationship with God and ourselves. All of these are important resting points in our lives. I found rest. She found rest. As a result, our perception of, reception of and existence in life is so much better.

Please understand the definition of rest, God's admonishment to rest, the purpose of rest and the power of rest. Yes, God has commanded us to rest. Yes, there is a purpose in resting and as you very well know, there is power associated with rest.

Like many of my friends, I too wake up racing. I realized not only my body, but also my mind was going 520 miles per hour. There was so much in my mental backpack.

There was my old job, my desire to want to be the supplier, my volunteerism, my misconception that I must attend every church function while I was three-fourths blind, sick and grieving over a 4-year old deceased love one. My immediate and feverish eagerness to serve distorted my spiritual vision, hearing and true assignment. I had not really focused on God's plan for me.

Is your plan for your life many tasks, within tasks wrapped up in one big task? When the day is over, have you done what God has appointed you to do or what you think *should* be done? How do you know? Has God told you to move or has someone else told you, you are good at it? (Whatever "it" is.) When did you take the time to listen? Have you so vastly and randomly spread all of you not realizing that the one God has chosen you to give to is left with a share only the size of a needle point? Have you poured out all that you have for miles and miles that the community God has designated to you remains unchanged by the mere sprinkles you left yesterday?

In order to be great, purposeful and effective stewards, we, like any religious or spiritual leader, prophet, political advocate, teacher, mom, dad, student, athlete, even farm land and bear, we must find rest in a quiet place that will help us hear what God has instructed us to do.

LESSON 5: Staying busy without intent helps no one. You must avoid being a busybody and find rest. According to Mother Theresa, it is in silence that we actually hear what God is telling us. Find that moment in your week or your day to sit and listen, receive and rejuvenate your soul. It is in that space, that you will be receptive to truth. I must add that resting is not a form of idleness. Resting allows you to hear what is being asked of you. It allows you to see what you are given purpose to do. Meditate on what action you should take and celebrate what is to come.

Rush

Pleading for a Buried Gift

As a grade-school child, I thought it evil to have such a "gift" placed upon me. I believed nothing good ever came of it. As a child, there was no clear context of what was given to me. I considered this gifted purpose intense punishment placed upon me even though I thought I did nothing wrong. This purpose did not seem like a gift at all, just an abnormally suffocating evil, too complex to tell and too psychotic to want to explain.

Until reaching my mid-20's, I never considered my purpose a gift, just a buried curse. Now I am opening my arms to all spiritual support. I am here I am burning incense, buying beaded necklaces I will never wear and searching for the right piece of fabric, quietly begging my ancestors to come back and promising them I'll listen. I envy Oprah's connection with the ancestors she calls upon before each business meeting. I prayed for God to give me my gift back and that I would work hard to serve in my gift the way God felt I should.

Looking back to my childhood, I realized one of my clear experiences was at an aunt's house. I recall my cousins and I were playing in the yard. Then I stopped. The RUSH came like a movie fast forwarding in front of me. My cousins, however, kept playing. I wasn't existing anymore, but my cousins were. I saw them moving around me like I was watching a 3D film. I felt like an energy, with no body, no image, no voice, yet clarity came about me and I knew. I knew one of my cousins would fall to my left and scrape her knee. She would cry and clutch her knee beneath the scar. Then the world started with me again. I was alive and present. Then my cousin fell, scraped her knee, began to cry, clutched her leg and adults ran out of the house. For days, I felt guilty, as if my thoughts are what caused my cousin's painful fate. However, Dean Radin, researcher and author, would call my episode "pre-feeling." Pre-feeling is the instance people *know* before the event has even happened yet. As for my reality, I learned this was actually a display of my gift, prophesy.

As a child, the most intense feelings of prophesy happened at night. Spirits came to my bedroom inching closer and closer to my bed, hovering over and around me, probably wondering when I'd ever peak from under the covers. I felt if I showed my face, they would suck my soul into the darkness only to take me to a place where I would always feel sad. During those moments, I would sleep during the day and lie awake at night. Though I didn't understand the first few times, I know now they were trying to tell me they are taking someone away. I knew this because each series of visits preceded a human death. At death, I was never sad. It was not until I became a young adult that I became sad from guilt, not from the death itself. It was the guilt of not preparing someone for what was about to happen.

The first time I told my cousin/guardian and her husband, they were more nonchalant than I thought. They waited until night time and checked into my room. My cousin's husband stood at my door one night for a few seconds staring at me. He tried to explain a life event I already know so well, death. He tried to comfort me with scriptural words and described to me a being I later came to love-God, God's plan for life and need for death. Both my cousin and her husband saw my spiritual episodes as copasetic. Their validation made me feel as if I was okay. When they expressed that, I no longer felt crazy. The last time the RUSH feeling was so intense while living with them was at their kitchen table. I had a sleepless night and knew this time it was okay to say.

Everyone was cooking, but me, bustling around in the kitchen. I made sure everyone was quiet before I spoke. "I'm sorry. Someone will die now," I said. And that's all I said. Everyone stopped, stared then carried on with their bustling. Then the phone rang. "She died," my cousin said slowly hanging up the phone. Everyone stared at me as if I was supposed to go into a spiritual convulsion. I said nothing else. I did nothing else. We all simply ate dinner. The woman who passed was not a blood relative, nor was she a close friend. I felt it was so wrong to place my spiritual consciousness in the realm of someone I didn't know. For that moment, I begged God to take away the gift. I no longer wanted to be the bearer of what I thought was "deadly news."

One day, I sat down and attempted to write about the process of this gift, since I couldn't verbally define how it feels. What I discovered in writing the piece, is that my feelings came out and so did the gifted purpose. Below are the words that came to me when writing.

I knew because

I'm grabbed by one arm around my stomach

The other arm presses my chest with a hand that bares

down on my shoulders

I knew because not being able to breathe wasn't painful

I knew because though I was entrapped I was not afraid

I knew because the thought of diving felt good

I knew because the thought of not knowing gave me

contentment

I knew because agreeing to jump, eyes closed, I would be

free

Free

Freely me and freely engulfed in uncertainty

I knew and no one else had to know. Me.

Those listening just had to know

I am made free in my uncertainty

I knew because

When I agree to dive and allow the embrace to let go of

me

I can then breathe, tell the message and ultimately just be.

When I read what I wrote, I noticed these words paused as

my thoughts paused. The words cut off where I wanted to

change how I felt or as my thinking changed. In that

writing, I demonstrated how I can use my gifted purpose and move to a more mentally peaceful space. Looking back, I see these words show I am also anxious and unknowing of what would happen, but they also show that I eventually trusted the gifted purpose given to me by God and all I have to do is simply release my hesitation and act on the instruction given to me.

As an adult, I am often told that this "gift" is given to individuals who have experienced a life trauma. For me, trauma is my life. At first I thought it was God's way of giving me testimonies I didn't ask for. Then I thought it was God's way of getting me to appreciate life. Now, I wonder if it is God's way of continuously preparing me for a greater purpose. Either way, I think God could have stopped at my momma and left the childhood migraines, brain tumor, going legally blind, skin cancer scare and discovered colon polyps out of the picture. I got it. I've been traumatized and I get it.

But now that I know and better understand my gifted purpose as a prophetess and know that my hunger for knowledge is so intense, I am here, quietly pleading to my

God to come forward, accept my apology and give me back my gift.

LESSON 6: Your gifted purpose may hurt, if you do not fully understand the context. We are human. Reach out to others to help coach, support and lead you to places of understanding along the way. It is okay to recognize that their support and acceptance also promotes your growth.

Hope LeNoir

Delightfully Twisted Events

Once I dreamed I was riding in a minivan. The minivan was a traditional size. It was familiar and so was the driver, my cousin, who had raised me since I was in sixth grade. It was only she and I in the van. I remember seeing her straightened hair with hints of grey strands. She navigated the wheel carefully, backing up closer and closer to what seemed like a small wooden building. I looked over my left shoulder and saw spirits peeking out through the window of a white shotgun house. They were not sensationalized ghosts in white sheets with large empty black holes as eyes. They were people, shaped like human bodies, just lighter, more ethereal, as if I was watching a 3D movie whose color had been faded out. My cousin's husband came out of the screen door on the side of the house. He was the only man there. He walked down the steps with a small folder and headed toward the minivan. Then he was gone, as if that were his only purpose.

I turned around, and my cousin was still navigating the van backward. I turned again and looked over my right shoulder and there I saw my female ancestors. They were

51

not washed out, but very vivid. They stood behind the minivan as if waiting for me to reach them.

"Stop," I spoke to my cousin. "Stop. We can't touch them."

I kept looking back with my right arm and hand resting on the back of the seat. Some of the women ancestors glared with a closed lip smile while others showed no expression at all. They all stood strong. Waiting. They were a black and brown group of people standing sporadically in the yard waiting for an arrival. They stood uninhibited, and calm, simply the presence of power with a sense of humility. The sight of my mother was fleeting. My grandmother was there too with a crown full of grey hair. There was an aunt there too with smooth golden skin and black-brown straightened hair. I didn't know her name, but somehow I knew she was my aunt. Somehow I knew all of the women there were my ancestors, but I could not call all by their name. Mudear, my aunt and former guardian, was among those who stood out. I remember her and I remembered her name.

"We can't touch them. We can't feel them either," I said to my cousin who was still backing the car up.

Suddenly the minivan's rear window was gone. Mudear took and caressed my hand as if showing a sign of gratitude. My last thought was, "She actually *did* touch me." It was then that I woke up.

My sister and I talk about our dreams all the time. I was so excited to tell her this one. Though *I* was usually the one attempting to interpret our dreams, this time I wanted my sister to give her thoughts. What did the white shotgun house mean? Why was John the only man there? Why was my cousin driving the minivan? Why is it that my ancestors and I could actually feel each other's touch?

"Your dream affirms what we are trying to do," my sister said. "They are grateful we are planning an event to honor the older women in our family. That makes me feel good. We're doing the right thing."

I smiled at the thought that my sister believed the women in our family, who had passed on, were communicating with me. She believed our ancestors were spiritually still here. For that, I was relieved. I inhaled and exhaled at knowing my ancestors really are here and they are indeed grateful for what we were about to do.

The event to honor the women in my family came, but never went away.   It was beautiful watching my elders sashay around in their purple and black clothing, salt and pepper hair, giggling and glowing. Even though it seemed impossible, their backs straightened even more as we served their brunch, gave their gifts and spoke of them as royalty. Surely, if my women ancestors were there, they were grateful too. I left the event knowing I had finally given my elders and ancestors a portion of the gifts they deserved.

After the event, I went on with my life, showing my appreciation, working, creating, building my relationship with God and volunteering my time. In so many ways, I still show appreciation to my ancestors.

One day, I walked into the nonprofit office where I volunteered ready for an educational meeting that turned out not to exist. The Program Specialist was there. He was a short man with a healthy frame. His name means "Protector." He told me I did not have to be there, but if I wanted to stay I could wait to see if anyone else showed up. If someone else came he would have a special session with us. The intent would be to talk about the mentoring program so this would not become an empty trip. I waited as he moved back and forth between rooms, checking his desk, looking out of the front door and peering out at people attending other meetings. He finally sat down in a chair in front of me and immediately it felt like several spirits entered the room. I giggled at the idea of all of my women ancestors surrounding me. While sitting immediately I felt the Protector knew my ancestors are there too. He leaned forward and held out his palms. I intuitively gave him my hands. He pretended to look at my nails, but I knew what he sensed.

"You are a special woman," he said. I chuckled inside. Though all men use that as a first liner, I knew this man was an intuitive, and he was hesitant because he wasn't sure I would receive. He went on to talk about his gift of communicating with ancestors, which I sensed he could do before he even spoke. It wasn't until he told me he could that I became intrigued. Finally, I thought, a line of substance. I think. Substance is what I was waiting for. He released my hand, leaned back and shooed something away with his hand.

"What?" I asked.

"They're trying to talk to me," he laughed out loud.

"What are they saying?" I leaned forward.

"I don't want to do this now," he said. "Not now, but they're here. They love you so much." I sighed in disappointment. I knew that part already.

"Do you do things for them?" he asked.

"What do you mean?" I was ready to learn all that he experiences and wondered if what he experiences will reveal to me what I can experience. I wanted spirits to talk to me. I wanted them to show themselves and give me knowledge to give others. In came the RUSH.

"Do you do things for them? Do you bring them things they like?"

"Sort of," I thought but was too embarrassed to share.

In this moment I developed a curiosity I had to appease. This would begin my journey to how various cultures learn from the gifts of their ancestors. This would be a part of a journey I may never forget. This would also be a journey that may never end.

LESSON 7: In lesson 6, I told you to reach out to others. This is an important part of lesson 7 as well. Learn from others. Despite their religion, position or level of insight, there is something to learn from others, even if it's perspective or to simply a point to disagree. There is a point of growth to be gained. All those seeking and discussing their purpose have one God or Spirit they believe in, therefore, be sure not to, as the Quran suggests, waist energy on the messenger. Instead, focus on the message and how it should or should not be a part of your purpose.

Hope LeNoir

Why *My* Personal Journey

There are so many books with so many tactical things, like why this and why that, and you have to feel this and feel that and you have to go that way. Then there are books that contradict and restrict the things we have been taught before, like follow your gifted purpose, but don't follow your gifted purpose. Then there is a perception of what purpose really means. Of course there are a lot of tests that can help you figure it out. And when I say figure it out, I mean uncover what your true destiny is, what your true happiness is and in what space that happiness really exists. These books even explain what it feels like when there are contradictory perspectives in environments that engulf you.

So I write this book to help you on that journey. I offer you a different twist to what you may have already read. For example, this book is not strictly quantitative and not strictly informational. This book puts context to discovering and embracing your gifted purpose while at the same time embracing life, emotions, statistics, and theories. This book encourages you to welcome confirmation of what it is you and I were put here to do. Yes, I talk about God. I refer to Christ. I quote the Quran. I mention The Spirit as well as ancestral Spirits. I share information I've learned from researchers like Tom Rath, Sir Ken Robinson and Mihaly Csikszentmihalyi. I sprinkle in educational pieces from pastors, writers and speakers like Tony Robbins, Rickie Rush, Isaac Malone and Rhonda Byrne. Everyone I've named is not absent in your experience, culture or tradition, and I find it admonishingly necessary to learn from all, even in perspective, in order to grow. This book is for the statistical. It is for the quantitative. It is for the qualitative persons. It is for spiritual persons. It is for the confused persons. It is for the person who likes inspiration and knowledge regarding their purpose. It is for people who are looking for something that touches them visually through words. I wrote this book because there is value about finding out what your gifted purpose is that will drive you to accomplish so many things for yourself and others. This book is an easy, but a different way to helping you tune in to your gifted purpose, embrace it and go with it, no matter how peculiar it may seem.

Yes, you are gifted and admonished to do certain things in your specific purpose. But just because you are gifted does not mean everything comes automatically and that you don't have to do anything to grow it. The truth is you can be gifted in a particular area, but you must always remember that a gift is just that. It doesn't mean it just goes into a corner to be seen every now and then or used every now and then. Again, a gift of purpose is something that should be taken care of and grown.

In the course of this book, *taken care of* means examined, stretched, continuously developed, used, polished off, grown and all through that there may have to be some alterations that fit as the environment changes. That does not mean your gift all together changes. It simply means the way you present your gift changes. It means how your gift is perceived by others changes. The message regarding your gifted purpose changes so that it is a gift you can share with other people who really need you to display your gifted purpose. What I share in so many speeches and writings about my gift are perspectives about the physiological, humanistic, and emotional aspects of discovering, experiencing, and using your gift toward a

61

larger purpose. For me, all of these perspectives came together in time and will continue to expand.

For example, I went through the *Strengths Finder* quiz and examined my top 5 strengths, one of which is Individualization. As I was looking at my top five, I realized how much they coincide with my spiritual gift. My spiritual gift, also known as "gifted purpose," is the gift of prophesy. In reading my stories, I took you through the journey of how I discovered my spiritual gift. I went through a lot of life changes. All through those it is apparent I have a gifted purpose to give people instruction and exhortation about specific elements of their lives.

I started out by telling you that as a child, when something was going to happen, I later realized that if I told that "somebody" that something was going to happen, life was so much easier for me emotionally. For example, the story of how I was a little girl and knew that one of my cousins was going to fall and hurt her knee even to the impact that it was going to bleed disturbed me. Telling her it was going to happen or even instructing her on ways to avoid it from happening would have relieved me and eventually my little cousin. What I told you are stories where I just have the strong urge to call a particular person and tell them the words that are given to me. Just by me telling the receiver, relieves me, even if I don't know or understand that is going to happen next.

For example, I moved to a new state, got a new job and opened a new bank account. I was introduced to a new banker who introduced himself and told me about the new account options. I opened the account and left very happy about my account decisions. The next day, I felt this disturbing feeling all about me. In the mist of the feeling, this banker kept coming to my mind. It was a feeling that something is going to happen. Something is *going* to happen. *Something is going to happen*, a voice in my mind repeated. It's not the, "What will happen?" It is the "it will happen." Something is going to hold tight of me until I release it to that person that keeps coming up in my mind. I don't know what's *going* to happen or what *has* been happening to him, but either way, I had to release this message to him.

I must say, initially it was frustrating. All I know is if I were to tell this person the words that were on my heart at that moment, then I would be released from whatever that is capturing me. For a long time, I dealt with it that way, knowing I would be released if I called that person and gave them a message as admonished.

I eventually called the banker and told him, "I know we just met, um, but there's something that I've got to tell you." In my mind, I'm thinking, *I don't care what you do with this "something" I got to tell you. What I do know is I've got to tell you to be released from whatever this is.* Sure, after the message is delivered, there is a curiosity of how the message has that impacted a person's life. Then there's the question, "What's the reality in it all?" I believed that in the experience, there was a reality for the receiver, but I had no idea what that reality was or would be for anybody that I talked to thus far.

I told the banker that everything was going to be okay. What he's going through right now, he didn't have to worry about it anymore. That it's going to work out. This issue that he has at home, he knows what it is, is going to work out. It's going to be okay and it's going to stay intact. I also told him "not to leave." To most people, this message seems very general.

I get the stories in the movies where audience members say, "Oh they could have said that to anybody. We all have our own issues at home." But if only you're in that moment would you be able to understand what's happening and how those feelings actually manifest themselves in your thoughts and in your body. It actually feels like a physical overtaking to me, but a mental clarity to people that don't expect it. As I've grown, the people I speak with hear what I have to tell them. They know exactly what it is that I'm talking about. So the receiver is consumed or filled with clarity.

When I shared the message for my professional banker, he listened quietly. I end by saying, "That's all I have to say to you. This is all I'm supposed to tell you. I hope I didn't scare you. You don't have to do anything with this. This is just the message I have for you."

At first, I told you I wanted to know what the message was about and what happened afterwards, but before talking to the banker, I've accepted that me telling the person is enough.

So he paused and said, "I know exactly what this is."

I responded, "Okay," then I paused. "Great," I said in my ready to end the conversation tone.

The banker continued by talking about his relationship with his wife and how at the kitchen table that morning, he thought it was all over between them. He talked about sitting in his office right now, repeatedly thinking, "I'm done. This relationship is over." He explained how me saying *don't give up, it's going to work out*, gave him a different confirmation. The banker told me he was a spiritual man, a strong believer in God and a typical member of a southern church. Traditional Christian church, that is. I believed him. His story held my curiosity. As described in my poem, I was released from the feeling of, *I've got to let this go*. This feeling of *I'm chained* no longer existed. This feeling of *I can't eat. I can't sleep. I can't think straight. I have to give this person a message* is gone. For me, that message doesn't always come out clearly in my mind. I just pick up the phone and talk to the receiver.

This went on for a long time with people I barely knew, just met, or hadn't established a relationship. I accepted that. I was okay, since my brother-in-law, who is a minister who specializes in talking about spiritual gifts, made it clear that a prophet is a person that gives direction or encourages. It's one or the other, instruction or good news. That's my part. That's all I have to do. It is up to the receiver to take the next step.

I began to accept that I don't really need to know the rest of the story. I don't need to know if it's relevant, because I trust that it is. I go on with my life knowing I gave something to someone that will help them maintain, grow or be lifted. Once the message is delivered, that which was laid on my heart has been released and now I can breathe. That which was laid on my heart, I have released it in the way that I should have. Everybody's life goes on.

I thought about the many things I have said to people, and realized my brother-in-law was right. It was instruction or it was good news, and I don't have to keep track of them to make sure they did what I said they should do, or check in to see if it's relevant or any of that stuff. I simply played my part. Follow up was not my calling, gift or the responsibility that was laid upon me. The instruction was given and my conflicted feeling was released and I was okay with that. This was similar to my top five strengths I referenced before, none of which described my strength as the ability to follow through or make sure recipients execute. My strengths do include, however, the ability to identify and instruct based on distinctions. (I will write more about my professional strengths in the next chapter.) I also accepted that I would not have this feeling or this admonishment laid upon me for family. I realize that I'm too close to my family. I realized my God would be kind enough and say, "This is what I've given her. She's done what I said. I'm not going to lay that on her to have these types of conversations with her family." At least that's what I thought God thought.

Then there was that night I slept and dreamed about my cousin. In the dream she I and her husband were in the car together. Her husband was driving. My cousin was on the passenger side. I was in the backseat. We were in a coupe with just enough room for my long legs in the back seat. I remember finally getting to our destination, though I'm not sure what the destination was. As a lucid dreamer, I was okay with not knowing the destination, because I realized it wasn't the focus of this journey. Next I remember my cousin-in-law getting out of the car and wondering why we had not done the same.

"Y'all get out," he says.

"No. No," I replied.

"Yeah. Y'all get out. We're here," he continued.

My response to him in the dream was, "I'm not moving, because my cousin can't move."

"Just get out," he says in his naturally calm voice. He came around to open the door for his wife.

"She cannot move. So she's not getting out of the car. Since she can't move, I'm not getting out of the car either," I said with my eyes stayed on my cousin.

Then I woke up from my dream.

I learned my lesson years ago not to call folks at 6:30 in the morning, so I waited anxiously. At about 7:30, when I knew my cousin's kids had woken my cousin up, I gave her a call. I asked if she had a few minutes. She did.

"Well, I have something to tell you," I said.

"Okay."

"Have you been to the doctor?" I asked.

"No. Not lately. My last visit went well though."

"Are you feeling okay?"

"Yeah, I'm feeling fine."

"For me, could you just go to the doctor?"

My cousin knows what I do and how I feel before things are about to happen.

She asks, "What is it?" It was the type of "what is it" that says, *I know you know something. I know you're feeling something. Tell me, what is it that you need to message?* I told my cousin about the dream. I said, "I want you to go to the doctor because something is going to prevent you from moving."

"Oh, I'm fine. Everything's okay. I don't think I need to go to the doctor," were my cousin's words.

Nevertheless, I'm sure you're reading this thinking, *Oh my God, she didn't go! What happened to her?* The situation turned out to be an illness that, since it was caught early, was not life threatening, and I am so happy about that.

My cousin did call me back that same afternoon and told me she was at the hospital in the emergency room. "After I talked to you, I felt numb," she said. "By the time I entered the emergency room, I couldn't walk. I couldn't move." I listened. She goes on to tell me what happened.

She ended up being in the hospital for a few days for something that had happened to her spine.

I'm grateful that God gave me that insight and admonished me to instruct. I'm glad that he chose me. Though this was about close family, I know why He chose me. He chose me because my cousin knows and understands and can appreciate the gifted purpose that I have. Most importantly, she can listen. My cousin listened and moved when she got an abnormal feeling. She got the treatment that she needed and I am so grateful and so happy for her.

LESSON 8: Be brave when it comes to growing and using your purpose. Know that you have a cause, a reason for existence and that reason is important. Trust that reason by believing goodness will come out in the end. Act on what is given to you. Dr. Martin Luther King, Jr. said it well when he said, "Faith is taking the first step even when you can't see the whole staircase." I challenge you to take that first step to move into your gifted purpose even when the outcome isn't clear to you yet.

Hope LeNoir

Wanting to Help

To get better at my gifted purpose, I often watch videos, listen to audios, attend conferences and read countless books. Like you, I have to hone my own skills to be of greater service to others. *Strengths Finder* is one of those tests that I took among many professional tests. This book stands out in particular, because I like how *Strengths Finder* focuses on your strengths, not your weaknesses. I've always been that person that doesn't want to spend a lot of time on things I'm not aligned to do. I appreciate that I am not designed or purposed to do everything, and you should accept the same about yourself. Understand, that yes both you and I are very capable, but not called to do certain things. Think about it, how can you be an arm, leg, neck and foot? Unless otherwise admonished, do not neglect your specific gift. So many others are waiting for you to live in your purpose in order to help their lives to not just move, but in many cases, move forward.

I started comparing Strengths Finder to my spiritual gift. I discovered my top strengths and my spiritual gift are alike. In other words, my professional strengths are right in line with my spiritual gift. This was confirmation of what I was put here to do. My purpose is to instruct, give good news and be able to identify the individualistic gems attached to each human being by seeing what makes them different and what can make them better. I suggest you do the same comparison as well. If it's your true gifted purpose, you will want to continuously grow it in many segments of your life for not just yourself, but for others around you. You will want to build it, research it, love it, figure it out and share it. Because of my growing discovery, I have professional one on one and group sessions about how my attendees' professional strengths are in line with their spiritual gifts. As a working professional in any environment, you should be aware of both.

I've given you quite a few examples of how I've discovered, grown and taken advantage of the RUSH of my gift in a spiritual environment. Now I'll share more of how the RUSH of my gift came in a corporate environment by sharing the story of an interview.

I entered the room prepared for a traditional interview. Traditionally, managers go in a room and ask lots of questions of one person. That's all I thought it should be. That's all I expected. I hoped this candidate would be an excellent choice, that I would be impressed her answers. I hoped that I would be in the room thinking, I like this person. I would love for her to be on my team. But that wasn't the case for this interview.

This is another example of how I felt the RUSH. Remember the RUSH is the excitement, the desire, the thrill, the wanting to help someone in a particular way so their outcome is better. To this end, let me tell you in detail about the interview.

I was sitting at the table when the young lady comes in. We do the traditional greeting. *Hi. How are you? You found the location okay?* Then we did the traditional introduction. *My name is Hope. I've been here for several years and have experiences in the following areas.* The other interviewing leader gave a similar introduction which included his journey at the company as well. And then we asked, *Will you tell us about yourself?*

This young lady hadn't graduated from college yet, but she is almost done. In her conversation, she told us she wasn't sure what it is she wanted to do. She stated she thought this company would be a good start, but she saw herself doing something different in the future. She wasn't sure what that "different" thing will be. She said she's trying to find herself. I became extremely energized. To the traditional interviewer, he or she would probably say, "Oh, my gosh. I don't have time for this. I need somebody who wants to be here. Who is excited about being here. Who wants to stay here. Who anticipates growing, but growing with our company and helping our company." This is where I am different. I felt a RUSH. I was thrilled that she wanted to find her professional self and I appreciated her honesty. But most of all, I wanted to help in her journey. I wanted to help her find that space where she felt fulfilled, included, like this is the place where she belongs. This is the place where she wants to develop. I so wanted to say to her, "Do you remember my name? Here's my number. You should call me. I want to share the message I am instructed to give you. I want to support you on that journey. I want to help you see your way, the right way." I wanted to stop the interview and help her on that journey to not only find her purpose in her professional life for herself, but also so she can help so many other people through her gifted purpose. Because the RUSH is so overwhelming, it's hard not to tell her what I'm thinking. Did I say it's hard to feel and identify my emotions? Outside of the RUSH, it's hard to express them. It's hard to explain exactly how I felt. Each day, I'm getting better at feeling and expressing. Right now, I best identify it as a RUSH. It seems as if I was surrounded by warmth. A boldness, greed, highness, oh wait. Greed would be a negative word. Let me start over. I was surrounded by warmth. I was surrounded by this strong desire to want to help. I was being inundated by this being that wants to support by implementing this need to use my gifted purpose and my skill to give direction. My gifted purpose is to help this young lady grow in her space. More importantly, I felt it. Confirmation. Confirmation to be in that space of direction. This is what I am destined to do. This is who and what I am.

I wonder what that woman is doing now. Did she find her place? Does she belong? What I can say is when all of the leaders got in a room together to make the final decision, that woman was not chosen for this role. They wanted someone who said, "This is the place I want to be and this is what I will do here." I can appreciate that. I can understand them wanting someone to want the same thing they want. Wanting someone who can grab the goals and have the same projection as they did. Yes, I can appreciate that.

Professional clarity was also confirmed while employed at another company. Here's the deal. I'm often asked to join in on executive conversations about professional development. Why? Because that's the place, at this point, where I've demonstrated I like to be. That's the place where I've shown expertise. That's the place where I have been a thought leader for organizations, so they've asked me to join.

I was asked to go talk to some executives about professional development in their company. I went to this meeting. Happy about it. Glad to be there. For some reason, I felt this will be another meeting with the intention to simply meet new people. Talk about stuff. Nice. So I went.

I lot of leaders were there, chit chatting before the meeting got started. We began our introductions. I gave my name and I explained what it is that I do. "My name is Hope. I am a professional coach. What I do is help people understand what their skills are, which determine what their desires are and identify where they are successful. I have to say, that's what I do and I do it well."

Then the executive started talking about professional development in the company. She talked about the different stages of the professional program she imagined and what her dream was to build that platform. I smiled and, believe it or not, the RUSH came. My whole body was filled with so much excitement, not for me, but just in the conversation itself. The RUSH was also about the thought of people growing professionally. I was engaged with new professional development programs being explored in the company. I was a part of that conversation. Even more importantly, I was deliberately asked to be a part of that conversation. This is where I think I should have felt proud. I could have felt thankful that I was chosen to be a part of that meeting. I think I should feel happy. I think I should feel a lot of positive things and I did.

The conversation itself thrilled me. It wasn't that I was a part of the conversation, but I was in the midst of the conversation. The conversation was a part of me. It was fascinating to know it was a part of who I am. I talked about things that I knew about, read about and experienced. I talked about what so many people are hungry to know. How can people grow professionally? How can professionals be satisfied by the things they do every day? I talked about what is it they can hug and claim as their own and why. What is it they can visualize and say, "You know what, I played a part in that effort. Not only did I play a part, but I am continuing to grow and learn and do more." For the company, I told them what the company needs to do to make sure the right people are in the right seats according to their strengths, purpose and passion.

The conversation had me excited. I am so glad to have been a part of this conversation, but I'm so glad this conversation was a part of me. Those thoughts came with the RUSH. This is how it feels when you identify your gifted purpose and recognize it is you and you are it and most of all, it is to help others bloom.

Though this book is ending, my journey will still continue. Throughout my life and throughout your life, there will be great stories to tell as you continue to identify and build your gifted purpose.

Remember the 8 Lessons learned in this book and how they relate to your journey to identify, accept and embrace your gifted purpose in a greater way.

Lesson 1: Be in every moment in your life, recognizing and appreciating what it gives to you

Lesson 2: Be aware of the hints detailing your gift

Lesson 3: Be receptive to the idea that your gifted purpose is not just about you

Lesson 4: Build an "I am worth it" and "I am valuable" mindset regarding your gifted purpose

Lesson 5: Commit time to be still and listen to your God for clear direction regarding your gifted purpose

Lesson 6: Be clear that pain may come with lack of understanding and that is a natural feeling. Look forward to heal and learn

Lesson 7: Be open to learning from others

Lesson 8: Be brave when it comes to both growing and using your gifted purpose

Benjamin Disraeli said it best when he said, "The greatest good you can do for another is not just share your own riches, but to reveal to him his own." I hope this book has given you relatable and easy ways to discover your own gifted purpose. I'll keep turning the page and telling you about my exciting, and very different journey. I hope you do the same for others too. Keep discovering, growing and celebrating the gifted purpose given to you!

Pen Your Gifted Purpose

Helpful Ways to Identify, Embrace and Put Your Gifted Purpose into Action

1. What is it you feel you have to do to be free? Write that here.

_____

_____

_____

_____

_____

_____

_____

_____

_____

_____

_____

_____

_____

_____

_____

2. When you wake up the next morning, write down what you want to give to the world ALL day.

_____

_____

_____

_____

_____

_____

_____

_____

_____

_____

_____

_____

_____

_____

_____

_____

_____

_____

3. The first time I heard God was when I laid still on my back in my empty apartment with outstretched arms. All I wanted to do was hear my God.

    Schedule a least three times this month (on different days), where you will commit to 15 minutes of being both mentally and physically still but, comfortable. Choose to have your 15 minutes in a quiet surrounding where nothing will disturb you but a 15 minute alarm. If you want more than 15 minutes, take more than 15 minutes. If you want to have this experience for more than three separate days, take more than three days. This is time with just you and God where the only intent is to listen then write down what you gained.

    DAY 1

    _____

    _____

    _____

    _____

    _____

    _____

Hope LeNoir

DAY 2

_____

_____

_____

_____

_____

_____

_____

DAY 3

_____

_____

_____

_____

_____

_____

_____

_____

4. What have you learned from others about your gifted purpose today?   What about yesterday? Where do you plan to learn more next week?

_____

_____

_____

_____

_____

_____

_____

_____

_____

_____

_____

_____

_____

_____

_____

_____

_____

5. What will you do to celebrate your gifted purpose now?

_____

_____

_____

_____

_____

_____

_____

_____

_____

_____

_____

_____

_____

_____

_____

_____

Now, put your purpose to use.

Hope LeNoir is the founder and owner of Rise and Fly ©, LLC, a business that helps professionals advance personally and professionally in their careers. Hope is a forward thinking Professional Strategist and Coach who has assisted hundreds with getting greater professional results and providing greater services to others. She has embraced several career journeys including being a professor, leader in the financial industry, professional in corporate citizenship, professional in children's television and much more. Hope has also been an inspirational speaker for an audience of thousands. Hope states, "My heart pounds when I help identify the challenge, see my clients get great results and watch them develop beyond what they ever imagined."

Made in the USA
Charleston, SC
20 March 2016